Raccoons for Kids
(Ringed Tails and Wild Ideas)

by Jeff Fair

NorthWord PRESS

Minnetonka, Minnesota

DEDICATION

To Mom, who put up with the clothesline capers,
and
To Dad, who caught the crayfish in Kellig Run, so long ago.

© 1995 by Jeff Fair
Photography © Alan and Sandy Carey

NorthWord Press
5900 Green Oak Drive
Minnetonka, MN 55343
1-800-328-3895

Designed by West 44th Street Graphics, Minneapolis, MN
Illustrations by John F. McGee

National Wildlife Federation® is the nation's largest conservation, education and advocacy organization. Since 1936, NWF has educated people from all walks of life to protect nature, wildlife and the world we all share.

Ranger Rick® is an exciting magazine published monthly by National Wildlife Federation®, about wildlife, nature, and the environment for kids ages 7 to 12. For more information about how to subscribe to this magazine, write or call: Ranger Rick Department, National Wildlife Federation, 8925 Leesburg Pike, Vienna, Virginia 22184, 1-800-588-1650.

NWF's World Wide Web Site http://www.nwf.org provides instant computer access to information about National Wildlife Federation, conservation issues and ideas for getting involved in protecting our world.

Library of Congress Cataloging-in-Publication Data

Fair, Jeff
    Raccoons for kids / by Jeff Fair.
      p.   cm.
    ISBN 1-55971-229-5
    1. Raccoons—Juvenile literature. [1. Raccoons.] I. Title.
    QL737.C26F35   1993   93-47298

Printed in Malaysia

Raccoons for Kids
(Ringed Tails and Wild Ideas)

by Jeff Fair

Whten I was about your age, I lived in a broad, green valley full of farms, where a kid could spend a whole summer catching butterflies and sneaking up on woodchuck burrows and banging on big old hollow trees to see what jumped out. A little river flowed through our valley. The maps called it Swatara Creek. We called it the Swatty, and we fished in it sometimes.

Our valley was pretty good country for raccoons, but so is almost all of North America. That includes where you live, unless you live in the middle of the desert, way up in the Rocky Mountains, or in northern Canada or Alaska. Raccoons like the same countryside most people do. They prowl the woods and stream banks. They sneak around farms and fields and even our own back yards. Sometimes. After dark.

Late one spring, when the air smelled like fishing and the grass smelled like baseball and school days dragged on forever, a little orphan came to my house for a visit. She wore a mask on her face and rings on her skinny little tail. From her perch in my pocket, she peered out over a pointed snout with a pretty keen nose at the end of it. She kept her ears perked up so she wouldn't miss a thing. That made her look worried. My Dad said that worrying is a sign of intelligence.

She moved into a box in the animal pen out back. Since raccoons are usually born in late April or May, I figured she was about two months old. That's just the age when her mom would have moved her and three or four brothers and sisters from the den she was born in—way up in a hollow tree—to a den near the ground, where Mom would start showing them the world. So the timing was just right for this box to be her den on the ground. It was up to me to show her around.

That first night I showed her how to drink milk out of a saucer. Then she tried to crack open my silver pocket watch in her teeth. Raccoons like shiny things because shiny things look wet, and wet things are often food for a raccoon. In fact, you can't keep a raccoon away from water. This one soon learned to operate the hose nozzle outside and the faucets inside the house. If she quietly disap-peared somewhere inside, we checked the plumbing first.

When it got late that evening, she didn't want to go out to her den. "Put her out anyway," my Mom said. "She'll learn." But instead, she learned to unhook the door of her pen. Raccoons learn fast, but they don't always learn what you want them to. They have their own wild ideas behind that mask.

How intelligent are raccoons? One scientist reported that raccoons are smarter than cats. That doesn't tell us too much. But he went on to say that raccoons can remember how to open difficult latches for a whole year, without even practicing. He said this proves that raccoons think, and that they actually have ideas. No kidding. I knew that.

Once I watched four fishermen teasing a pair of raccoons. They tied a fish head to a fishing line, cast it to the edge of the woods, reeled it back, and howled with laughter when the raccoons followed it. The fishermen thought they were really playing a joke on the raccoons. But the fishermen weren't watching their tent, where three other raccoons opened every cooler and made off with all the good stuff. Talk about ideas.

After three or four days, my little visitor learned to play in the daytime and go to bed when I did. Raccoons are normally nocturnal, or active at night. But they often change their schedules so they don't miss a meal. They wake up to eat clams on the beach during morning low tide, or to accept an afternoon handout on somebody's back porch.

I checked on the little raccoon each night from my bedroom window by shining a flashlight into her pen. Her eyes glowed greenish-gold and bright as a pair of electric lights. Most nocturnal animals have a special part in each eye that helps them see at night and reflects the beam of a lantern or a headlight. Raccoons probably can't see colors, only black and white. But that's about all you can see anyway under the starlight, where raccoons do most of their hunting.

Raccoons are put together in such a way that their hind legs carry most of their weight. That means they can save their front paws for grabbing and feeling things. They have five long toes on each little black foot, and they walk on the soles of their feet just like you do.

Their hind feet are as tender as yours, but a raccoon's front feet have four times as many nerves as your hands to feel with. When those paws have nothing else to do, a raccoon will just sit and rub them together, as though it was thinking up another wild idea. If a raccoon put its paw in yours, it would feel to you like a tiny human hand wearing the softest, finest deerskin glove.

My little friend followed me everywhere I went. She thought she was human, and I thought she was mine.

She spoke in sweet little trills, softly when she was happy and loudly when she wanted attention. She saved her little cackle for times when things weren't going just right.

I buckled a puppy collar around her neck. She didn't seem to mind. Raccoons are fairly tolerant. She'd even walk on a leash, sort of, as long as you went where she wanted to go.

16

One day in July, Mom clipped the leash to her and walked up to Grandpa's house on the hill. She tied the leash to a tree and went in to visit. When she came out, the leash was still there, attached to the collar. But there was no raccoon in the collar. Mom was worried. She ran home, looking up into every tree. When she got to the pen out back, she found the little raccoon snug in her box.

We shouldn't have been surprised. At her age, about three months, wild raccoons start following their mothers to look for food. But they usually get scared and change their minds on the first few trips and scurry back to their den to wait for Mom. That's exactly what this little raccoon did. Some wild ideas are planted in an animal's brain even before it's born. These ideas we call instincts.

Wild raccoon kits follow their mother farther and farther from the den each time. A mother raccoon takes good care of her kits and doesn't lose many. She carries a straggler by the skin on the back of its neck. By late summer, young raccoons are weaned and know how to find their own meals. Some of them go off on their own, but most wait until the next spring.

A yearling raccoon may move 30 miles away—and sometimes more than 100. It's a raccoon's one big chance to travel.

I worried that someday my little companion would run away. I was afraid of losing her. That's how you feel when you have something that isn't really yours.

Raccoons are talented climbers. Few other mammals can climb down a tree head-first after they climb up the tree. My little friend learned in the lilac bushes. Next she climbed the skinny dogwood tree Dad had just planted, then climbed up the big maples as far as I'd let her. She climbed the living room drapes, leaving little toenail tracks in them, which made Mom frown. Sometimes she'd run across the yard in her comical, bounding run, then run right up my leg and my back, all the way to my shoulder. That left little toenail tracks in me sometimes, but I didn't mind.

She'd climb up onto the clothesline like an acrobat in a circus tent. Then she'd hang from my socks, trying to look pitiful and in need of rescue. It was her wild idea of a game. It was good climbing practice, too.

Raccoons climb trees to pick apples and to find their dens, which can be as high up as a sixth-story window. They choose tree cavities that are protected from rain and hard to fall out of.

Raccoons usually have more than one den, and they aren't all in trees. A second-hand woodchuck hole will do. Dens in the ground are warm in winter and cool on hot summer days. Raccoons also den in hollow logs, junk piles, lumber stacks, barns, attics, sheds, chimneys, and abandoned cars like the rusty old Rambler in my Grandpa's field. Raccoons are adaptable. They see the things humans build, then they get wild ideas.

Raccoons eat just about anything that a bird, a fish, or somebody's uncle might think of as food. They eat fruits, berries, grains, insects, snails, slugs, worms, snakes, lizards, turtles, ducks, rabbits, mice, clams, mussels, apple cores, uneaten oatmeal, and lost lollipops. They eat eggs right out of alligator nests in southern swamps and steal eggs out of hawk nests 50 feet up in trees. Raccoons eat grass and beetles in the summer, when both are chewier. In the autumn, like bears, they eat acorns and other wild nuts to fatten up for the winter. Corn from cornfields and gardens is a treat. They like sweet corn best on the night before your mom decides to pick it.

Once I saw my little ring-tailed friend grab a swallowtail butterfly in mid-flutter. She ate that, too. She chewed it for a full minute. She chewed everything at least a hundred times. That must be instinctive, because she never saw me do that.

Then she swallowed the swallowtail.

But raccoons do their best hunting in shallow water. They catch small fish and their all-time favorites: crayfish. They have been known to feast on whole frogs, but they unwrap toads and throw away the bitter skin. Raccoons tend to avoid salamanders—but really, who likes to eat salamanders?

One day Dad said someone should teach this little raccoon how to catch crayfish. Dad was thinking ahead. That evening we loaded ourselves and the swallowtail swallower into the Studebaker, and Dad drove us to a little creek where he caught crayfish hundreds of years ago when he was a kid. Crayfish sneak around under rocks. If you can catch a crayfish, you can catch just about anything in shallow water.

How you catch crayfish by hand is a big secret. What you have to do is find one, sneak up behind it with your hand under-water and your thumb and pointer finger almost together like a clothespin, take aim, get real brave (that's the tough part at first), and jab down like lightning so your thumb and finger pin down the crayfish and pinch its claws up next to its head, where they can't hurt you.

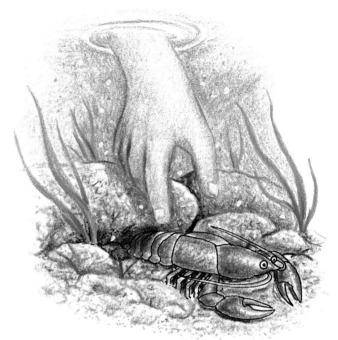

25

Dad caught a couple of little ones and gave them to the raccoon. She chewed them up like grasshoppers. Then Dad tossed a huge one to her on the shore. She reached for it, got pinched, tried again, got pinched again, and finally got the idea. She sat back now, sort of half-closed one eye and wrinkled her nose, and crunched down on the crayfish's head with those sharp, canine teeth. That stopped the pinching. She ate the tail first. Then she rubbed her front paws together, thought up a wild idea, and waded in all the way up to her belly hairs.

She found her prey by feel, patting the stream bottom lightly with her forepaws while peering off toward the horizon. She looked like a piano player gazing around at the audience while his fingers were finding all the right keys. She never looked at a crayfish until she had ahold of it. The little ones she ate right there in the water. The big ones she brought to shore for special handling.

We hadn't really taught her anything, of course. Raccoons know by instinct how to fish. We just brought up the idea.

In the wild, a raccoon spends almost every day in its own neighborhood, or what biologists call its home range. It would take you about an hour to walk across a raccoon's home range, which might be along a stream, in the woods, or right in town. It would take longer in places where food is scarce, because the raccoon would have to hunt farther to find enough to eat.

Raccoons spend most of their time alone, but their home ranges overlap. If they didn't, raccoons wouldn't get together to share raccoon ideas, and no little raccoons would be born. We all have to share some ideas if we want to survive. Nature operates that way, at least for us mammals.

Why do raccoons wear masks? To fool each other? Not likely. Raccoons recognize each other in their neighborhoods without using names or faces. They probably use smell more than anything. Every raccoon smells just a little bit different. We humans all smell different, too, but our noses aren't as sensitive as those pointy raccoon noses, so we don't have to go around sniffing each other. Lucky for us.

So why the mask? Nobody knows for sure. Maybe it's just one of those wild ideas, a touch of whimsy from Old Mother Nature. Like your ear lobes, for example, or those four, five, six, or even seven dark rings around a raccoon's tail.

Raccoons have another way of keeping tabs on each other. Where their paths cross, several raccoons may leave their droppings. So each raccoon, as he passes, learns what the others have eaten. Feed one or two raccoons at your porch this summer, and you may have 50 raccoons visiting you next year. Word gets around.

Now here's a warning: Raccoon droppings sometimes carry the eggs of parasitic worms that would just as soon hatch and grow up inside your intestine. They're enough to make you sick. So don't do any close-up research on raccoon droppings. You don't need to know that much about raccoons.

Just where do you find raccoon paths? Good question. Bears and foxes and deer leave tracks on our dirt roads and hiking paths, but we don't see many raccoon tracks there. Raccoons don't follow human trails. They make their own, and you have to look for them.

Check for tracks out by the corn, or over by the hen house if you have one. Mush around the marsh on a warm winter day near a big hollow tree. But the best place to look for raccoon tracks is in the smooth mud along the side of a stream.

Raccoon tracks look like tiny human hand and foot prints. Their hind feet make the longer tracks, just like yours do. Sometimes their tracks are in pairs: the right rear foot leaves a track next to the left front foot, and the other pair does just the opposite. It's a trick raccoons play. You have to watch one walk to see how they do it.

Raccoon tracks often tell stories about what they eat. If you find some by the creek, look for minnow tails, crayfish claws, and toad wrappers. These are raccoon leftovers.

You don't have to hold your nose around many wild animals, raccoons included. My ring-tailed friend always smelled as clean and fresh as a winter coat, except for one time in my neighbors' house when their dog snapped at her. That poodle didn't even know he was risking his life. A raccoon can lick any dog. Even so, most raccoons would rather run away than tear apart a poodle. Not that a raccoon can run very fast. A ninth-grader with his sneakers on can outrun a full-grown raccoon, but he usually doesn't get the chance. The raccoon sees a tree or a hole or a rusted-out Rambler, gets one of those wild ideas, and disappears.

But that day my little friend was cornered. She growled (first time I ever heard that), raised the long hairs on her back, waved her tail, bared her teeth, and lowered her snout. She suddenly smelled more like a skunk than a raccoon, and it made me want to stay away from her. She was ready for a dogfight, but we gave the poodle a break and went home.

Not too many predators mess with raccoons. Great horned owls and eagles and bobcats may catch young raccoons. Cougars, wolves, and coyotes occasionally grab an adult. Alligators get a few slow ones, but they don't get many. So wild raccoons usually live a long time for an animal of their size: maybe 7 to 12 years, or about as long as their teeth last. With human care and soft food, raccoons have lived to be 16.

By late autumn, my little friend had gobbled enough food to add a layer of fat for the winter. She weighed close to 15 pounds. Adults this time of year average 20 or 30 pounds, about as much as a big Thanksgiving turkey while it's still walking around being a turkey. My little friend was two feet long now, but a third of her was tail. The fur coat she had shed last summer had grown back thick and shiny.

Raccoon pelts, or hides, were once considered a prize. Native Americans made coats out of them, with the tails left on as fancy decoration. Some American colonists in the 1700s were paid their salaries in raccoon skins.

Back then, people used raccoon fat to make a salve for burns and cuts and, like most anything else they could shoot or trap, they ate the raccoon meat. It was a wild idea pioneers got when they were hungry. Some people still eat raccoon meat. You should cook it, the old-timers say, just like you'd cook a possum. It's supposed to taste a lot like lamb. I tried it once. It tasted more like possum to me.

After the first snow fell, my little friend dozed in her den-box and only came out to eat during warm spells. Raccoons don't really hibernate like bears, but they stay in bed through the coldest weather and live off their fat for days at a time. Up north, they may lose ten pounds of their body weight just staying warm. That can be half a raccoon!

Some of them save heat by sharing their dens and curling up together. The record so far is 23 raccoons—eight adults and 15 young—in one winter den. All pressed together, they added up to as much mammal as a healthy black bear. And they had at least 23 times as many wild dreams.

One night in March, a caterwauling out by the pen woke me up. In my flashlight beam I saw two pairs of greenish-gold eyes. Another raccoon had come to visit. He must have whispered some wild raccoon idea to my little friend. She was never the same after that. She didn't look worried any more. She just looked thoughtful. Dad said this was a sign of maturity. That made sense. Like any healthy, well-fed one-year-old raccoon in the wild, she had grown ready for the special company of a mate.

She tried to run away twice that spring. The second time I barely caught her, and before either of us could think, she bit my hand.

"It's time for her to go back to the woods where she belongs," Dad said.

That evening we locked her in her box and drove her back to the Swatty. We carried her down to the creek, and Dad let her out.

She climbed her first tree of freedom, and I climbed the trail back to Dad's Studebaker. I hoped for a moment that she might climb back down the tree and run up the trail after us. Then I remembered that wild raccoons don't follow human trails. Dad said she was climbing higher so she could watch us leave, but way down inside I was pretty sure she had a wilder idea.

That was many summers ago, but I still see raccoon tracks down by the Swatty when I go back. I like to imagine the little raccoon kits down there with worried looks on their faces, fetching crayfish out of the creek and climbing their trees of freedom. And I know the most important thing I ever did for that little ring-tailed orphan was to let her go free. Maybe that's a wild idea. I wonder where that came from?

MORE WILD (RACCOON) IDEAS —

Raccoons are famous for washing their food. The only problem is, they don't really do that. They don't need to. Most of their food is clean enough already. What people have mistaken as washing isn't washing at all. It's "dabbling," or feeling around for food underwater. It's a very old habit, fixed in that little raccoon brain with all those other wild ideas.

A long time ago, a scientist gave raccoons their scientific name: Procyon lotor. If that looks like Greek to you, that's because it is. It sounds like Greek, too: PRO-see-on LOW-tore. From way back in time, Procyon means "related to dogs," which raccoons are. And lotor means "the washer," which really isn't true.

The Algonquian Indians who lived in what is now Virginia knew their animals better, but they didn't know Greek. They called this animal *arakunem*, which means "he scratches with his hands." The early English settlers took the middle part of that word, rakun, and turned it into "raccoon."

Because raccoons are happy to benefit from human crops, buildings, and garbage, the raccoon population has been getting bigger for 50 years. The disappearance of many of its predators (including the local raccoon trapper) helped, too.

But too many raccoons, like too many people, can be a nuisance. They steal chickens and swipe sweet corn. They pry open garbage cans and break into bird feeders. More raccoons eat more eggs, including the eggs of birds that can't afford to lose them. Loons, for example.

Crowded by their own numbers, raccoons suffer outbreaks of diseases called distemper and rabies. They also move into cities, where they scratch around in gutters and dabble in storm drains. They've moved into parts of the desert, where they can now find water—mostly in swimming pools and bird baths—where it never was before.

Raccoons have also moved farther north in Canada, to places where the local Algonquian natives had never seen one before and had no name for it. So we gave them ours. "Raccoon," we said. "Oh?" they said. "Rakun?"

Raccoons can adjust to our civilization, but they don't understand human rules. Like most wild animals, raccoons usually don't make good pets. But that's okay. It's more fun to see a raccoon running free than it is to watch one pacing back and forth in a cage, trying to exercise its wild ideas.

Still want to get to know raccoons better? Keep your eyes peeled out there between your back door and the wilderness. That's where your home range overlaps with theirs.